Stop Overthinking

*Master Your Mind, Reduce Stress,
and Live a Happier Life*

R. Sharma

**"You are not a victim of
your thoughts. You have
the ability to redirect
them."**

Copyright © [2024] by [R. Sharma]

Contact Info:-
www.facebook.com/WriterRSharma

Welcome to "Stop Overthinking: Master Your Mind, Reduce Stress, and Live a Happier Life." This book is a labor of love and dedication, born out of a deep desire to help those who, like myself, have struggled with the relentless cycle of overthinking.

Overthinking can be an overwhelming force, robbing us of our peace, clarity, and joy. It can make even the simplest decisions seem daunting and create an endless loop of worry and self-doubt. I know this all too well, having walked this path myself. But through this journey, I discovered that it is possible to break free from the grips of overthinking and reclaim control over our minds and lives.

This book is a compilation of strategies, insights, and practical tools that have helped me and countless others. It is my sincere hope that these pages will provide you with the guidance and encouragement you need to navigate your own journey towards mental clarity and emotional well-being.

As you read through the chapters, remember that you are not alone. Each step you take towards understanding and managing your thoughts is a step towards a more peaceful and fulfilling life. Be patient with yourself, celebrate your progress, and know that every small victory is a significant achievement.

Thank you for choosing to embark on this journey with me. I am honored to be a part of your path towards overcoming overthinking and finding greater happiness and balance in your life. Together, we can break free from the chains of overthinking and create a brighter, more serene future.

With heartfelt gratitude and best wishes,

R. Sharma

Stop Overthinking

Table of Contents

1. **Introduction**

2. **Understanding Overthinking**

3. **Breaking the Cycle of Overthinking**

- ✓ Mindfulness and Awareness
- ✓ Cognitive Behavioral Techniques
- ✓ Developing a Growth Mindset

4. **Practical Strategies to Stop Overthinking**

- ✓ The Power of Journaling
- ✓ Setting Boundaries and Priorities
- ✓ Time Management and Productivity Tips

5. **Building Mental Resilience**

- ✓ The Role of Self-Compassion
- ✓ Stress Management Techniques
- ✓ Healthy Lifestyle Choices

6. Mindfulness and Meditation Practices

- ✓ Introduction to Mindfulness
- ✓ Guided Meditation Exercises
- ✓ Incorporating Mindfulness into Daily Life

7. Dealing with Anxiety and Fear

- ✓ Understanding Anxiety
- ✓ Techniques for Managing Anxiety
- ✓ Facing and Overcoming Fears

8. Creating a Support System

- ✓ The Importance of Social Support
- ✓ Building Healthy Relationships
- ✓ Seeking Professional Help When Needed

1. Introduction

What is Overthinking?

Overthinking is the process of continually analyzing, replaying, and second-guessing thoughts and experiences, often to the point of causing mental and emotional distress. It involves dwelling excessively on past events or worrying about the future, leading to a cycle of repetitive and unproductive thoughts. While it's natural for everyone to reflect on past experiences or plan for the future, overthinking becomes problematic when it interferes with daily functioning, decision-making, and overall well-being.

The essence of overthinking lies in its unproductive nature. Instead of leading to solutions or new insights, it often results in increased anxiety, self-doubt, and a sense of being stuck. For instance, a person might replay a conversation repeatedly, wondering if they said something wrong, or they might obsess over a decision, fearing the potential consequences of making a mistake. This constant rumination can be mentally exhausting and emotionally draining.

Overthinking is not a diagnosis in itself, but it is commonly associated with anxiety disorders, depression, and other mental health conditions. It's a symptom that can exacerbate these issues, making it harder for individuals to cope with their thoughts and emotions effectively.

The Consequences of Overthinking

The consequences of overthinking are far-reaching, impacting various aspects of an individual's life. Here are some of the most common effects:

1. **Increased Anxiety and Stress**: Overthinking often leads to heightened levels of anxiety and stress. The constant worrying and rumination can trigger the body's

stress response, leading to physical symptoms such as headaches, muscle tension, and fatigue. Over time, this chronic stress can take a toll on physical health, contributing to issues like heart disease, digestive problems, and weakened immune function.

2. **Impaired Decision-Making**: When individuals overthink, they can become paralyzed by indecision. The fear of making the wrong choice or the need to analyze every possible outcome can prevent them from making timely decisions. This indecision can lead to missed opportunities and a sense of regret, further fueling the cycle of overthinking.

3. **Negative Impact on Mental Health**: Overthinking is closely linked to mental health conditions such as depression and anxiety disorders. The persistent negative thoughts and self-criticism can

erode self-esteem and contribute to feelings of hopelessness and helplessness. In severe cases, overthinking can lead to suicidal ideation or self-harm.

4. **Strained Relationships**: Overthinking can also strain relationships with family, friends, and colleagues. Individuals who overthink may misinterpret others' words or actions, leading to misunderstandings and conflicts. They may also seek constant reassurance from others, which can become burdensome and frustrating for their loved ones.

5. **Reduced Productivity and Performance**: Overthinking can interfere with focus and concentration, making it difficult to complete tasks efficiently. This reduced productivity can affect academic or work performance,

leading to feelings of inadequacy and frustration.

6. **Sleep Disturbances**: Overthinking can disrupt sleep patterns, making it hard for individuals to fall asleep or stay asleep. The racing thoughts and worries can keep them awake at night, leading to insomnia and sleep deprivation. Poor sleep quality, in turn, exacerbates anxiety and stress, creating a vicious cycle.

7. **Decreased Quality of Life**: Overall, overthinking diminishes the quality of life. It robs individuals of their peace of mind, preventing them from fully enjoying the present moment. The constant mental chatter and worry can overshadow positive experiences and lead to a sense of dissatisfaction with life.

How This Book Will Help

This book aims to provide practical strategies and insights to help individuals break free from the cycle of overthinking and regain control over their thoughts and emotions. By understanding the nature of overthinking and its consequences, readers will be better equipped to recognize and address their own patterns of rumination.

Throughout the book, readers will find:

1. **Evidence-Based Techniques**: The strategies and techniques presented in this book are grounded in scientific research and proven therapeutic approaches. From mindfulness practices to cognitive-behavioral techniques, readers will learn effective methods to manage and reduce overthinking.

2. **Practical Exercises**: Each chapter includes practical exercises and activities designed to help readers apply the concepts to their own

lives. These exercises will encourage self-reflection, promote mindfulness, and build resilience against overthinking.

3. **Real-Life Examples**: The book features real-life examples and case studies to illustrate how overthinking manifests in different situations and how others have successfully overcome it. These stories provide inspiration and reassurance that change is possible.

4. **Comprehensive Approach**: Addressing overthinking requires a holistic approach that considers mental, emotional, and physical well-being. This book covers various aspects of mental health, including stress management, self-compassion, and lifestyle choices, to support readers in their journey towards a balanced and fulfilling life.

5. **Long-Term Strategies**: Overcoming overthinking is not a quick fix but a gradual process of developing new habits and perspectives. This book offers long-term strategies to help readers maintain their progress and continue growing even after they have completed the book.

By the end of this book, readers will have a deeper understanding of overthinking and its impact on their lives. They will gain practical tools and techniques to manage their thoughts more effectively, reduce anxiety and stress, and improve their overall mental well-being. Most importantly, they will be empowered to take control of their minds and lead a more peaceful and fulfilling life.

2. Understanding Overthinking

The Science Behind Overthinking

Overthinking is a complex phenomenon that involves various cognitive processes and brain functions. To understand it fully, it's essential to delve into the science behind how our brains work and why we might fall into the trap of overthinking.

Cognitive Processes Involved

1. **Rumination and Reflection**: Rumination is the repetitive focus on the symptoms of distress and its possible causes and consequences. Unlike reflection, which can be constructive, rumination is unproductive and often exacerbates negative feelings. Reflection involves a balanced examination of past

experiences to gain insights and learn from them, whereas rumination traps individuals in a loop of negative thinking.

2. **Cognitive Biases**: Cognitive biases are systematic patterns of deviation from norm or rationality in judgment. Common biases associated with overthinking include:

   o **Catastrophizing**: Expecting the worst possible outcome in any given situation.

   o **All-or-Nothing Thinking**: Seeing situations in black-and-white terms, without recognizing any middle ground.

   o **Overgeneralization**: Drawing broad, negative conclusions based on a single event.

3. **Executive Function and Decision-Making**: The prefrontal cortex, the part of the brain responsible for executive functions, plays a crucial role in decision-making and regulating thoughts. Overthinking can overwhelm this area, leading to decision paralysis and an inability to move forward.

Neurological Basis

1. **Brain Activity**: Research using neuroimaging techniques like fMRI has shown that overthinkers often exhibit heightened activity in the prefrontal cortex and the amygdala. The prefrontal cortex is involved in complex thought processes, while the amygdala processes emotions like fear and anxiety. This increased activity can make it difficult to disengage from negative thoughts.

2. **Neurotransmitters**:
   Neurotransmitters like serotonin, dopamine, and norepinephrine play a significant role in mood regulation and cognitive processes. Imbalances in these chemicals can contribute to anxiety, depression, and overthinking. For instance, low serotonin levels are often linked to mood disorders and excessive worry.

3. **Default Mode Network (DMN)**:
   The DMN is a network of brain regions that are active when the mind is at rest and not focused on the outside world. It is associated with self-referential thinking and mind-wandering. Overactivity in the DMN can lead to excessive introspection and rumination, contributing to overthinking.

Psychological Theories

1. **Cognitive-Behavioral Theory**:
   This theory suggests that our

thoughts, feelings, and behaviors are interconnected. Overthinking is seen as a pattern of maladaptive thinking that leads to negative emotions and unhelpful behaviors. Cognitive-behavioral therapy (CBT) aims to break this cycle by challenging and changing unhelpful thought patterns.

2. **Metacognitive Theory**: This theory focuses on how individuals think about their thinking. It suggests that people who overthink have negative beliefs about their thoughts (e.g., "I cannot control my worry") and positive beliefs about the value of worrying (e.g., "Worrying helps me prepare for the worst"). These metacognitive beliefs perpetuate overthinking.

3. **Attachment Theory**: According to this theory, early attachment experiences with caregivers shape our future relationships and

coping mechanisms. Individuals with insecure attachment styles may be more prone to overthinking as a way to seek control and predictability in their relationships.

Common Triggers and Causes

Overthinking can be triggered by various internal and external factors. Understanding these triggers and causes can help individuals identify and address the root of their overthinking patterns.

Internal Triggers

1. **Personality Traits**: Certain personality traits, such as perfectionism, high sensitivity, and a tendency towards introspection, can predispose individuals to overthinking. Perfectionists often strive for flawless performance

and fear making mistakes, leading to excessive analysis and worry.

2. **Self-Esteem Issues**: Low self-esteem and self-doubt can fuel overthinking. Individuals with low self-worth may constantly seek validation and fear judgment from others, leading them to overanalyze their actions and decisions.

3. **Past Experiences**: Traumatic or negative experiences from the past can leave a lasting impact and trigger overthinking. People who have experienced failure, rejection, or criticism may replay these events in their minds, trying to understand what went wrong and how to avoid similar situations in the future.

4. **Mental Health Conditions**: Anxiety disorders, depression, and other mental health conditions are closely linked to overthinking.

These conditions can amplify negative thoughts and make it challenging to break free from the cycle of rumination.

External Triggers

1. **Stressful Situations**: High-stress situations, such as major life changes, work pressure, or relationship problems, can trigger overthinking. When faced with uncertainty or difficulty, individuals may turn to overthinking as a way to gain a sense of control.

2. **Environmental Factors**: Living in a high-pressure environment or having a demanding job can contribute to overthinking. Constant exposure to stressors can keep the mind in a state of hypervigilance, making it difficult to relax and let go of worries.

3. **Social Influences**: Social interactions and comparisons can

also trigger overthinking. In the age of social media, constant exposure to others' highlight reels can lead to feelings of inadequacy and self-doubt, prompting individuals to overanalyze their own lives.

4. **Cultural and Societal Expectations**: Cultural and societal norms can shape how individuals perceive themselves and their achievements. Pressure to meet certain standards or conform to societal expectations can lead to overthinking, especially when individuals feel they are falling short.

Recognizing the Signs of Overthinking

Recognizing the signs of overthinking is the first step towards addressing and managing it. While everyone overthinks occasionally, chronic overthinking can have detrimental effects on mental health and overall well-being. Here are some common signs to watch for:

Cognitive Signs

1. **Constant Worrying**: Persistent worrying about future events or outcomes, even when there is no immediate threat or reason for concern, is a hallmark of overthinking. This worry often centers on "what if" scenarios and worst-case outcomes.

2. **Replaying Past Events**: Overthinkers frequently replay past events in their minds, analyzing what they could have done differently and second-guessing their actions. This can lead to feelings of regret and guilt.

3. **Indecisiveness**: Difficulty making decisions is a common sign of overthinking. Individuals may overanalyze every option and

potential outcome, leading to decision paralysis and an inability to take action.

4. **Perfectionism**: Striving for perfection and fearing mistakes can contribute to overthinking. Perfectionists often set unrealistically high standards for themselves and obsess over minor details.

Emotional Signs

1. **Anxiety and Stress**: Overthinking is closely linked to anxiety and stress. The constant mental activity and worry can trigger the body's stress response, leading to physical symptoms such as tension, headaches, and fatigue.

2. **Mood Swings**: Overthinkers may experience frequent mood swings, oscillating between periods of intense worry and temporary relief. These mood changes can

affect their ability to focus and maintain emotional stability.

3. **Low Self-Esteem**: Overthinking often involves self-critical thoughts and doubts about one's abilities and worth. This can erode self-esteem and lead to feelings of inadequacy and insecurity.

4. **Irritability**: The mental exhaustion caused by overthinking can result in irritability and frustration. Individuals may become easily annoyed or upset, especially when their thoughts are interrupted.

Behavioral Signs

1. **Procrastination**: To avoid the stress and anxiety associated with making decisions or taking action, overthinkers may resort to procrastination. They may delay tasks or put off important decisions, leading to increased stress in the long run.

2. **Seeking Reassurance**: Overthinkers often seek reassurance from others to validate their thoughts and decisions. This constant need for validation can strain relationships and make them overly dependent on others' opinions.

3. **Avoidance Behavior**: Avoiding situations that trigger overthinking is another common behavior. Individuals may avoid social interactions, challenging tasks, or new experiences to reduce their anxiety and stress.

4. **Overworking**: Some overthinkers cope by immersing themselves in work or other activities to distract from their thoughts. While this can provide temporary relief, it often leads to burnout and increased stress.

Physical Signs

1. **Sleep Disturbances**: Overthinking can interfere with sleep patterns, leading to difficulties falling asleep or staying asleep. Racing thoughts and worries can keep individuals awake at night, resulting in insomnia and fatigue.

2. **Physical Tension**: Chronic overthinking can manifest as physical tension, such as headaches, muscle aches, and tightness in the shoulders and neck. This tension is often a result of the body's stress response.

3. **Appetite Changes**: Overthinking can affect appetite, leading to changes in eating habits. Some individuals may lose their appetite, while others may turn to food for comfort and overeat.

4. **Fatigue**: The mental and emotional strain of overthinking can cause fatigue and low energy levels. Overthinkers may feel

constantly tired and lack the motivation to engage in daily activities.

Strategies for Recognizing and Addressing Overthinking

1. **Mindfulness Practice**: Mindfulness involves staying present and fully engaging with the current moment. Practicing mindfulness can help individuals recognize when they are overthinking and gently redirect their focus to the present.

2. **Journaling**: Writing down thoughts and feelings can provide clarity and help individuals identify patterns in their overthinking. Journaling can also serve as a release for pent-up emotions and reduce mental clutter.

3. **Cognitive Restructuring**: This technique involves challenging and changing negative thought

patterns. By identifying cognitive distortions and replacing them with more balanced thoughts, individuals can reduce overthinking.

4. **Setting Time Limits**: Allocating a specific amount of time for worrying or analyzing can help contain overthinking. Once the time is up, individuals can redirect their focus to more productive activities.

5. **Relaxation Techniques**: Relaxation techniques such as deep breathing, progressive muscle relaxation, and meditation can help calm the mind and reduce the physiological symptoms of overthinking.

6. **Seeking Support**: Talking to a trusted friend, family member, or therapist can provide a different perspective and help individuals

process their thoughts and feelings more effectively.

7. **Engaging in Physical Activity**: Regular physical activity can reduce stress and improve mood. Exercise releases endorphins, which are natural mood boosters, and helps divert attention from overthinking.

By recognizing the signs of overthinking and implementing strategies to address it, individuals can break free from the cycle of rumination and regain control over their thoughts and emotions. This journey requires patience and practice, but with commitment and perseverance, it is possible to lead a more peaceful and fulfilling life.

3. Breaking the Cycle of Overthinking

Mindfulness and Awareness

Mindfulness and awareness are powerful tools in the fight against overthinking. By focusing on the present moment and becoming more aware of our thoughts and feelings, we can interrupt the cycle of rumination and develop healthier thinking patterns.

Understanding Mindfulness

Mindfulness is the practice of paying attention to the present moment without judgment. It involves being aware of our thoughts, feelings, and sensations as they arise, and accepting them without trying to change or control them. This acceptance helps us to observe our thoughts from a distance, reducing their power over us.

Benefits of Mindfulness

1. **Reduced Stress and Anxiety**: Mindfulness helps to calm the mind and body, reducing the physiological and psychological symptoms of stress and anxiety. By focusing on the present moment, we can break free from the cycle of worry and rumination that fuels these conditions.

2. **Improved Emotional Regulation**: Mindfulness enhances our ability to regulate our emotions by increasing our awareness of our emotional states. This awareness allows us to respond to our emotions more skillfully, rather than reacting impulsively.

3. **Enhanced Focus and Concentration**: By training the mind to stay present, mindfulness improves our ability to concentrate and focus on the task at hand. This can lead to increased productivity and better decision-making.

4. **Greater Self-Awareness**: Mindfulness fosters a deeper understanding of ourselves, including our thoughts, feelings, and behaviors. This self-awareness is the foundation for personal growth and self-improvement.

Mindfulness Practices

1. **Breathing Exercises**: Focusing on the breath is a simple yet effective way to practice mindfulness. By paying attention to the sensation of the breath as it enters and leaves the body, we can anchor ourselves in the present moment.

   - **Basic Breathing Exercise**: Find a comfortable position and close your eyes. Take a deep breath in through your nose, feeling your abdomen rise. Exhale slowly through your mouth, feeling your abdomen fall. Continue to breathe deeply and rhythmically, paying attention to the sensation of each breath.

2. **Body Scan Meditation**: This practice involves systematically focusing on different parts of the body, bringing awareness to any sensations or tension.

   o **Body Scan Exercise**: Lie down in a comfortable position and close your eyes. Start by focusing on your toes, noticing any sensations or tension. Gradually move your attention up through your feet, legs, abdomen, chest, arms, and head. Take your time with each body part, observing without judgment.

3. **Mindful Eating**: Eating mindfully involves paying full attention to the experience of eating, including

the taste, texture, and smell of the food, as well as the sensations in the body.

- o **Mindful Eating Exercise**: Choose a small piece of food, such as a raisin or a piece of chocolate. Before eating, take a moment to observe the food, noticing its color, texture, and shape. Slowly bring the food to your mouth, paying attention to the movement of your hand and arm. Place the food in your mouth and chew slowly, savoring the taste and texture. Notice any sensations in your body as you eat.

4. **Walking Meditation**: This practice involves walking slowly and mindfully, paying attention to the sensations of each step and the environment around you.

- o **Walking Meditation Exercise**: Find a quiet place where you can walk undisturbed. Begin walking slowly, focusing on the sensation of your feet making contact with the ground. Pay attention to the movement of your legs, the rhythm of your breath, and the sounds around you. If your mind wanders, gently bring your focus back to the act of walking.

Cultivating Awareness

1. **Mindful Journaling**: Writing down your thoughts and feelings can increase your awareness of your mental and emotional states. Mindful journaling involves writing without judgment or censorship, allowing your thoughts to flow freely.

- **Mindful Journaling Exercise**: Set aside 10-15 minutes each day to write in a journal. Focus on your current thoughts, feelings, and experiences. Write without worrying about grammar or structure. Use this time to explore your inner world and gain insight into your thought patterns.

2. **Mindfulness in Daily Activities**: Incorporate mindfulness into your daily routines, such as brushing your teeth, washing dishes, or taking a shower. By bringing full attention to these activities, you can practice mindfulness throughout the day.

   - **Mindful Activity Exercise**: Choose a daily activity, such as washing dishes. As you perform the activity, focus on the sensations, movements, and sounds involved. Notice the feeling of the water on your hands, the texture of the dishes, and the sound of the water running. If your mind wanders, gently bring your focus back to the task.

3. **Awareness of Thoughts**: Pay attention to your thoughts as they arise, without getting caught up in them. Observe your thoughts as if you were watching clouds pass by in the sky.

   - **Thought Observation Exercise**: Sit quietly and close your eyes. When a thought arises, notice it without judgment. Label the thought (e.g., "worry," "planning," "self-criticism") and then let it go. Return your focus to your breath or the present moment. Repeat this process whenever a new thought arises.

Cognitive Behavioral Techniques

Cognitive Behavioral Therapy (CBT) is a widely used therapeutic approach that focuses on changing unhelpful thinking patterns and behaviors. CBT techniques can be highly effective in reducing overthinking and improving mental well-being.

Understanding CBT

CBT is based on the idea that our thoughts, feelings, and behaviors are interconnected. By identifying and challenging negative thought patterns, we can change the way we feel and behave. CBT involves practical, goal-oriented techniques that can be applied in everyday life.

Key CBT Techniques

1. **Cognitive Restructuring**: This technique involves identifying and challenging cognitive distortions, which are irrational and unhelpful thoughts.

   - **Cognitive Restructuring Exercise**: Start by identifying a negative thought, such as "I always mess things up." Examine the evidence for and against this thought. Consider alternative perspectives and generate a more balanced thought, such as "I have made mistakes, but I also have many successes."

2. **Thought Records**: Thought records are a tool used to track negative thoughts, identify cognitive distortions, and develop more balanced thinking.

   - **Thought Record Exercise**: Create a thought record

with the following columns: Situation, Emotion, Automatic Thought, Evidence For, Evidence Against, and Balanced Thought. When you experience a negative thought, fill in each column to analyze and reframe the thought.

3. **Behavioral Experiments**: These involve testing the validity of negative thoughts through real-life experiments.

   - **Behavioral Experiment Exercise**: Identify a negative thought, such as "If I speak up in a meeting, people will think I'm stupid." Design an experiment to test this thought, such as sharing an idea in a meeting and observing the reactions. Record the outcome and evaluate whether the original thought was accurate.

4. **Exposure Therapy**: This technique involves gradually facing feared situations to reduce anxiety and overthinking.

   o **Exposure Therapy Exercise**: Create a hierarchy of feared situations, starting with the least anxiety-provoking and gradually working up to the most challenging. Begin with the least feared situation and gradually expose yourself to each situation, using relaxation techniques to manage anxiety.

5. **Problem-Solving**: This involves identifying problems, generating potential solutions, and implementing the best solution.

- o **Problem-Solving Exercise**: Define a specific problem you are facing. Brainstorm a list of potential solutions without evaluating them. Evaluate the pros and cons of each solution and choose the best one. Create an action plan to implement the chosen solution and monitor the results.

6. **Mindfulness-Based CBT**: This integrates mindfulness practices with traditional CBT techniques to enhance awareness and reduce overthinking.

- o **Mindfulness-Based CBT Exercise**: Combine mindfulness meditation with cognitive restructuring. Begin with a mindfulness meditation to calm the mind. Then, use cognitive restructuring to challenge negative thoughts that arise during the meditation.

Developing a Growth Mindset

A growth mindset is the belief that our abilities and intelligence can be developed through effort, learning, and perseverance. This mindset contrasts with a fixed mindset, which assumes that our abilities are static and unchangeable. Developing a growth mindset can help individuals overcome overthinking by fostering resilience and a positive attitude towards challenges.

Understanding the Growth Mindset

The concept of the growth mindset was developed by psychologist Carol Dweck. According to Dweck, individuals with a growth mindset embrace challenges, learn from criticism, and persist in the face of setbacks. They see effort as a path to mastery and believe that their abilities can be developed through dedication and hard work.

Benefits of a Growth Mindset

1. **Increased Resilience**: A growth mindset promotes resilience by encouraging individuals to view challenges and failures as opportunities for growth. This resilience helps to reduce the impact of negative thoughts and overthinking.

2. **Improved Performance**: Individuals with a growth mindset are more likely to set and achieve goals, as they believe in their ability to improve and succeed. This leads to increased motivation and productivity.

3. **Enhanced Learning and Development**: A growth mindset fosters a love of learning and a willingness to take on new challenges. This openness to

learning can lead to personal and professional development.

4. **Better Relationships**: A growth mindset promotes empathy and understanding, as individuals recognize that everyone has the potential to grow and change. This leads to healthier and more supportive relationships.

Strategies for Developing a Growth Mindset

1. **Embrace Challenges**: View challenges as opportunities to learn and grow, rather than threats to your abilities.

   o **Challenge Exercise**: Identify a challenging situation you are currently facing. Write down the potential benefits and learning opportunities that this challenge presents. Commit to approaching the challenge with a positive attitude and a willingness to learn.

2. **Learn from Criticism**: Use feedback and criticism as valuable information to improve and develop, rather than as personal attacks.

   o **Criticism Exercise**: Reflect on a piece of constructive criticism you have received. Write down what you can learn from this feedback and how you can apply it to improve. Focus on the specific actions you can take, rather than dwelling on negative emotions.

3. **Celebrate Effort**: Recognize and celebrate the effort you put into tasks, regardless of the outcome. This reinforces the belief that effort leads to improvement.

   o **Effort Exercise**: At the end of each day, write down

three things you did well, focusing on the effort you put in. Reflect on how this effort has contributed to your growth and development.

4. **Reframe Failure**: View failure as a natural part of the learning process and an opportunity to gain valuable insights.

   o **Failure Exercise**: Think about a recent failure or setback you experienced. Write down what you learned from this experience and how it has helped you grow. Identify specific actions you can take to apply these lessons in the future.

5. **Set Growth-Oriented Goals**: Set goals that focus on learning and development, rather than on outcomes or achievements.

- **Goal-Setting Exercise**: Identify a skill or area you want to develop. Set a specific, measurable, achievable, relevant, and time-bound (SMART) goal related to this area. Break the goal down into smaller, manageable steps and track your progress.

6. **Practice Self-Compassion**: Treat yourself with kindness and understanding when you encounter setbacks or make mistakes. Recognize that growth and improvement take time and effort.

  - **Self-Compassion Exercise**: When you experience a setback, write a compassionate letter to yourself. Acknowledge your feelings and remind yourself that everyone makes mistakes and faces challenges. Focus on what you can learn from the experience and how you can move forward.

By incorporating mindfulness, cognitive behavioral techniques, and a growth mindset into your daily life, you can break the cycle of overthinking and develop healthier, more productive thinking patterns. These practices require commitment and consistency, but with time and effort, you can achieve greater mental clarity, emotional stability, and overall well-being.

4. Practical Strategies to Stop Overthinking

The Power of Journaling

Journaling is a powerful tool for managing overthinking. It provides a structured outlet for expressing thoughts and emotions, helping to clarify and process them. By externalizing internal dialogue, journaling can reduce mental clutter and foster self-awareness.

Benefits of Journaling

1. **Clarification of Thoughts**: Writing down thoughts helps to organize and clarify them. This process can lead to a deeper understanding of one's feelings and concerns, making it easier to identify patterns and triggers of overthinking.

2. **Emotional Release**: Journaling serves as a safe space for expressing emotions. This emotional release can reduce stress and anxiety, providing a sense of relief and catharsis.

3. **Problem Solving**: By articulating problems and brainstorming

solutions in a journal, individuals can gain new perspectives and identify actionable steps to address their concerns.

4. **Self-Reflection**: Regular journaling fosters self-reflection, enabling individuals to track their progress, recognize personal growth, and celebrate achievements.

5. **Mindfulness and Presence**: Journaling encourages mindfulness by focusing attention on the present moment. This practice can interrupt the cycle of rumination and promote a more balanced mindset.

Types of Journaling

1. **Free Writing**: This involves writing continuously without worrying about grammar, punctuation, or structure. Free writing allows thoughts to flow

freely, capturing raw emotions and ideas.

- **Exercise**: Set a timer for 10-15 minutes and write without stopping. Don't censor or edit your thoughts. Simply let your mind wander and capture whatever comes to mind.

2. **Prompt-Based Journaling**: Using prompts can provide structure and focus to journaling sessions. Prompts can be questions, statements, or themes that guide the writing process.

   - **Exercise**: Choose a prompt, such as "What am I grateful for today?" or "What are my current challenges and how can I overcome them?" Write for 10-15 minutes, exploring the prompt in depth.

3. **Gratitude Journaling**: This involves writing about things you are grateful for. Gratitude journaling can shift focus from negative thoughts to positive aspects of life.

   o **Exercise**: Each day, write down three things you are grateful for. Reflect on why these things are meaningful to you and how they contribute to your well-being.

4. **Reflective Journaling**: Reflective journaling involves analyzing past experiences and learning from them. This type of journaling can provide insights into behavior patterns and emotional responses.

   o **Exercise**: Think about a recent experience that had a significant impact on you. Write about what happened, how you felt, and what you learned from the experience. Consider how you can apply these lessons in the future.

5. **Goal-Setting Journaling**: This involves setting and tracking personal goals. Goal-setting journaling can provide motivation and accountability, helping to turn aspirations into reality.

   - **Exercise**: Write down a specific goal you want to achieve. Break the goal into smaller, manageable steps and create an action plan. Regularly update your journal with your progress, challenges, and reflections.

Integrating Journaling into Daily Life

1. **Establish a Routine**: Set aside a specific time each day for journaling. Consistency is key to making journaling a habit and reaping its long-term benefits.

2. **Create a Comfortable Environment**: Choose a quiet, comfortable space for journaling. Minimize distractions and create an atmosphere that fosters relaxation and introspection.

3. **Be Honest and Authentic**: Write honestly and authentically, without worrying about judgment or criticism. Your journal is a private space for self-expression and exploration.

4. **Review and Reflect**: Periodically review your journal entries to identify patterns, progress, and areas for growth. Use these reflections to inform your personal development and decision-making.

Setting Boundaries and Priorities

Setting boundaries and priorities is essential for managing overthinking and maintaining mental well-being. Clear boundaries protect your time and energy, while well-defined priorities ensure that you focus on what truly matters.

The Importance of Boundaries

1. **Protection of Time and Energy**: Boundaries help protect your time and energy from being depleted by unnecessary or unproductive activities. This protection is crucial for maintaining focus and preventing burnout.

2. **Reduction of Stress**: Clear boundaries reduce stress by creating a sense of control and predictability. Knowing your limits and sticking to them can prevent feelings of overwhelm and anxiety.

3. **Improved Relationships**: Boundaries enhance relationships by fostering mutual respect and understanding. They help prevent misunderstandings and conflicts, promoting healthier interactions.

4. **Enhanced Self-Care**: Setting boundaries is an act of self-care. It involves prioritizing your needs and well-being, ensuring that you have the resources to take care of yourself.

Strategies for Setting Boundaries

1. **Identify Your Limits**: Reflect on your personal limits and identify areas where you need boundaries. Consider your time, energy, and emotional capacity.

   o **Exercise**: Make a list of situations or activities that drain your energy or cause stress. Identify specific boundaries that could mitigate these effects.

2. **Communicate Clearly**: Clearly communicate your boundaries to others. Be assertive and direct, explaining your needs and expectations without apology or justification.

- **Exercise**: Practice communicating a boundary with a trusted friend or family member. Use "I" statements to express your needs (e.g., "I need time to myself in the evenings to recharge").

3. **Learn to Say No**: Saying no is an essential part of setting boundaries. It's important to recognize that you cannot do everything and that it's okay to decline requests that do not align with your priorities.

- **Exercise**: Practice saying no in a firm but polite manner. For example, "I appreciate the invitation, but I'm unable to attend this time."

4. **Set Consequences**: Establish consequences for when your boundaries are violated.

Consistent enforcement of boundaries reinforces their importance and encourages others to respect them.

- o **Exercise**: Identify a boundary and determine a reasonable consequence for its violation. Communicate this consequence to those involved.

5. **Prioritize Self-Care**: Make self-care a priority by setting boundaries that protect your time and energy for activities that nourish and rejuvenate you.

- o **Exercise**: Schedule regular self-care activities, such as exercise, hobbies, or relaxation, and set boundaries to protect this time from interruptions.

The Importance of Priorities

1. **Focused Attention**: Priorities help focus your attention on what truly matters. By identifying your most important goals and tasks, you can allocate your time and energy more effectively.

2. **Reduced Overwhelm**: Clear priorities reduce feelings of overwhelm by providing a roadmap for decision-making. Knowing what to focus on can prevent the paralysis that often accompanies overthinking.

3. **Increased Productivity**: Prioritizing tasks enhances productivity by ensuring that you work on the most important and impactful activities. This focus can lead to greater achievement and satisfaction.

4. **Balanced Life**: Priorities help create balance in your life by ensuring that you allocate time and energy to different areas, such

as work, relationships, and personal growth.

Strategies for Setting Priorities

1. **Identify Core Values**: Reflect on your core values and what is most important to you. Use these values as a guide for setting priorities.

   o **Exercise**: Make a list of your core values, such as family, health, career, and personal growth. Rank these values in order of importance and use them to guide your decision-making.

2. **Set Specific Goals**: Define specific, measurable, achievable, relevant, and time-bound (SMART) goals. Clear goals provide direction and focus, making it easier to prioritize tasks.

   o **Exercise**: Write down a SMART goal for each of

your core values. Break each goal into smaller, manageable steps and create an action plan.

3. **Use the Eisenhower Matrix**: The Eisenhower Matrix is a tool for prioritizing tasks based on their urgency and importance. It helps identify which tasks to focus on, delegate, or eliminate.

   o **Exercise**: Create an Eisenhower Matrix with four quadrants: Urgent and Important, Not Urgent but Important, Urgent but Not Important, and Not Urgent and Not Important. Categorize your tasks into each quadrant and prioritize accordingly.

4. **Regularly Review and Adjust**: Regularly review and adjust your priorities to ensure they align with your current goals and

circumstances. Flexibility is key to maintaining balance and focus.

- o **Exercise**: Set aside time each week to review your priorities and goals. Reflect on your progress and make any necessary adjustments.

5. **Limit Distractions**: Minimize distractions that interfere with your ability to focus on priorities. Create a conducive environment for productivity and set boundaries to protect your focus.

- o **Exercise**: Identify common distractions in your environment and implement strategies to reduce or eliminate them. For example, turn off notifications on your phone or create a dedicated workspace.

Time Management and Productivity Tips

Effective time management and productivity strategies are essential for overcoming overthinking and achieving your goals. By managing your time wisely, you can reduce stress, increase efficiency, and create a sense of accomplishment.

The Importance of Time Management

1. **Enhanced Focus**: Time management helps to enhance focus by allocating specific time blocks for tasks and activities. This focus can prevent distractions and improve productivity.

2. **Reduced Stress**: Effective time management reduces stress by creating a sense of control and predictability. Knowing what to expect and having a plan in place can alleviate anxiety.

3. **Increased Efficiency**: By prioritizing tasks and managing

time effectively, you can accomplish more in less time. This efficiency leads to greater productivity and a sense of achievement.

4. **Improved Work-Life Balance**: Time management helps to create a balance between work and personal life by ensuring that you allocate time for both. This balance is crucial for overall well-being and satisfaction.

Time Management Techniques

1. **Pomodoro Technique**: The Pomodoro Technique involves working for a set period (typically 25 minutes) followed by a short break (5 minutes). This technique promotes focus and prevents burnout.

   o **Exercise**: Set a timer for 25 minutes and work on a specific task. When the timer goes off, take a 5-

minute break. Repeat this cycle four times, then take a longer break (15-30 minutes).

2. **Time Blocking**: Time blocking involves scheduling specific blocks of time for different tasks and activities. This technique helps to allocate focused time for important tasks.

   o **Exercise**: Create a daily or weekly schedule, dividing your time into blocks for specific tasks and activities. Stick to your schedule as closely as possible, adjusting as needed.

3. **Prioritization Matrix**: Use a prioritization matrix (such as the Eisenhower Matrix) to categorize tasks based on their urgency and importance. This tool helps to identify which tasks to focus on and which to delegate or eliminate.

- o **Exercise**: List your tasks and categorize them into four quadrants: Urgent and Important, Not Urgent but Important, Urgent but Not Important, and Not Urgent and Not Important. Focus on tasks in the Urgent and Important quadrant first.

4. **Batching**: Batching involves grouping similar tasks together and completing them in one session. This technique reduces the time lost in switching between different types of tasks.

   - o **Exercise**: Identify similar tasks that can be batched together, such as responding to emails or making phone calls. Allocate specific time blocks for these batches and complete them in one session.

5. **Setting SMART Goals**: Setting SMART goals (Specific, Measurable, Achievable, Relevant, Time-bound) provides clear direction and focus for your time and efforts.

    o **Exercise**: Write down a specific goal and ensure it meets the SMART criteria. Break the goal into smaller, manageable steps and create an action plan. Allocate time blocks for each step.

6. **Limiting Multitasking**: Multitasking can reduce efficiency and increase errors. Focus on one task at a time to improve productivity and quality of work.

    o **Exercise**: Identify a task that requires your full attention. Set a timer and focus solely on that task until the timer goes off.

Avoid switching to other tasks during this time.

Productivity Tips

1. **Minimize Distractions**: Create a conducive environment for productivity by minimizing distractions. Turn off notifications, create a dedicated workspace, and set boundaries to protect your focus.

   - **Exercise**: Identify common distractions in your environment and implement strategies to reduce or eliminate them. For example, use noise-canceling headphones or set specific times for checking emails and messages.

2. **Take Regular Breaks**: Taking regular breaks is essential for maintaining focus and preventing burnout. Use techniques like the

Pomodoro Technique to incorporate breaks into your work routine.

- Exercise: Schedule regular breaks into your daily routine. During breaks, engage in activities that relax and rejuvenate you, such as stretching, walking, or meditating.

3. **Practice Mindfulness**: Mindfulness can improve productivity by enhancing focus and reducing stress. Incorporate mindfulness practices into your daily routine to stay present and focused.

- Exercise: Set aside time each day for mindfulness meditation. Focus on your breath and bring your attention to the present moment. Use mindfulness to stay centered and focused throughout the day.

4. **Delegate and Outsource**: Delegating tasks to others can free up time for more important activities. Identify tasks that can be delegated and assign them to capable individuals.

   - **Exercise**: Make a list of tasks that can be delegated or outsourced. Identify individuals or resources that can handle these tasks and communicate your expectations clearly.

5. **Use Productivity Tools**: Utilize productivity tools and apps to manage tasks, track progress, and stay organized. Tools like to-do lists, calendars, and project management software can enhance efficiency.

   - **Exercise**: Explore productivity tools and

choose one that fits your needs. Use the tool to create a to-do list, set reminders, and track your progress on tasks and projects.

6. **Reflect and Adjust**: Regularly reflect on your time management and productivity practices. Identify areas for improvement and make necessary adjustments to optimize your efficiency.

   o **Exercise**: Set aside time each week to review your productivity and time management practices. Reflect on what worked well and what could be improved. Make adjustments to your schedule and strategies as needed.

By incorporating journaling, setting boundaries and priorities, and utilizing time management and productivity techniques, you can break the cycle of overthinking and achieve greater mental clarity, focus, and well-being. These practices require consistency and commitment, but with time and effort, they can lead to a more balanced and fulfilling life.

5. Building Mental Resilience

The Role of Self-Compassion

Self-compassion is the practice of treating yourself with the same kindness, understanding, and support that you would offer to a friend. It is an essential tool for managing overthinking, as it promotes a healthy relationship with yourself and reduces the negative impact of self-criticism and rumination.

Benefits of Self-Compassion

1. **Reduces Self-Criticism**: Self-compassion helps to reduce self-criticism by encouraging a more supportive and understanding inner dialogue. This shift can alleviate the harsh judgment and negative self-talk that often fuel overthinking.

2. **Promotes Emotional Resilience**: Practicing self-compassion enhances emotional resilience by fostering a sense of inner strength and stability. It enables you to cope with difficult emotions and setbacks more effectively.

3. **Improves Mental Well-Being**: Self-compassion is associated with improved mental well-being, including lower levels of anxiety and depression. It creates a more positive and nurturing mental environment, which is conducive to managing overthinking.

4. **Encourages Personal Growth**: By treating yourself with kindness and understanding, you create a safe space for personal growth and self-improvement. Self-compassion allows you to learn from mistakes and challenges without fear of harsh self-judgment.

Practicing Self-Compassion

1. **Mindful Awareness**: Mindful awareness involves being present with your thoughts and feelings without judgment. It helps you to recognize moments of self-criticism and respond with self-compassion.

   o **Exercise**: Practice mindful awareness by taking a few minutes each day to sit quietly and observe your thoughts and emotions. When you notice self-critical thoughts, gently acknowledge them and redirect your focus to a more compassionate inner dialogue.

2. **Self-Kindness**: Self-kindness involves treating yourself with warmth and understanding, especially during times of difficulty or failure. It means offering yourself the same support and care that you would offer to a friend.

   - **Exercise**: When you experience a setback or make a mistake, practice self-kindness by speaking to yourself in a gentle and supportive manner. For example, say to yourself, "It's okay to make mistakes. I'm doing my best, and I will learn from this experience."

3. **Common Humanity**: Common humanity involves recognizing

that suffering and imperfection are part of the human experience. It helps to counter feelings of isolation and self-blame by reminding you that everyone faces challenges.

- **Exercise**: Reflect on a difficult experience and remind yourself that you are not alone in facing challenges. Think about others who have gone through similar situations and draw strength from the shared human experience.

4. **Self-Compassionate Writing**: Writing can be a powerful tool for cultivating self-compassion. It allows you to express your thoughts and feelings in a supportive and non-judgmental way.

- **Exercise**: Write a compassionate letter to

yourself. Describe a difficult situation you are facing and offer yourself words of encouragement and support. Focus on expressing understanding and kindness towards yourself.

5. **Self-Compassion Break**: A self-compassion break is a short practice that involves pausing and offering yourself compassion in moments of stress or difficulty.

   o **Exercise**: When you feel overwhelmed or stressed, take a self-compassion break. Place your hand over your heart, take a few deep breaths, and silently say to yourself, "This is a moment of suffering. Suffering is a part of life. May I be kind to myself."

Stress Management Techniques

Stress is a common trigger for overthinking, and effectively managing stress is crucial for breaking the cycle of rumination. By incorporating stress management techniques into your daily routine, you can reduce the impact of stress and promote a more balanced and calm mindset.

The Importance of Stress Management

1. **Reduces Physical Symptoms**: Chronic stress can lead to physical symptoms such as headaches, muscle tension, and fatigue. Managing stress can alleviate these symptoms and improve overall physical health.

2. **Enhances Emotional Well-Being**: Effective stress management improves emotional well-being by reducing anxiety, irritability, and mood swings. It creates a more

stable and positive emotional state.

3. **Improves Cognitive Function**: High levels of stress can impair cognitive function, leading to difficulties with concentration, memory, and decision-making. Managing stress can enhance cognitive performance and mental clarity.

4. **Promotes Better Sleep**: Stress often interferes with sleep, leading to insomnia or poor-quality sleep. Stress management techniques can improve sleep patterns and contribute to overall well-being.

Stress Management Techniques

1. **Deep Breathing**: Deep breathing is a simple and effective technique for reducing stress and promoting relaxation. It involves taking slow, deep breaths to calm the nervous system.

- **Exercise**: Practice deep breathing by inhaling slowly through your nose, filling your lungs with air, and exhaling slowly through your mouth. Repeat this process for a few minutes, focusing on the sensation of your breath.

2. **Progressive Muscle Relaxation**: Progressive muscle relaxation involves tensing and relaxing different muscle groups in the body. It helps to release physical tension and promote relaxation.

- **Exercise**: Start by tensing the muscles in your feet and holding the tension for a few seconds. Then, slowly release the tension and relax. Move up through your body, tensing and relaxing each muscle group.

3. **Mindfulness Meditation**: Mindfulness meditation involves focusing your attention on the present moment without judgment. It helps to reduce stress by promoting a sense of calm and presence.

   o **Exercise**: Set aside time each day for mindfulness meditation. Sit quietly, focus on your breath, and gently bring your attention back to the present moment whenever your mind wanders.

4. **Physical Activity**: Regular physical activity is a powerful stress reducer. Exercise releases endorphins, which are natural mood enhancers, and helps to reduce tension and anxiety.

   o **Exercise**: Incorporate physical activity into your daily routine. Choose activities that you enjoy, such as walking, jogging, yoga, or dancing, and aim for at least 30 minutes of exercise each day.

5. **Visualization**: Visualization involves imagining a peaceful and relaxing scene. It can help to reduce stress by creating a mental escape from stressful situations.

   o **Exercise**: Find a quiet place and close your eyes. Imagine a serene and calming place, such as a beach or a forest. Visualize the sights, sounds, and smells of this place, and allow yourself to relax.

6. **Time Management**: Effective time management can reduce stress by creating a sense of control and predictability. It helps to prioritize tasks and allocate time for relaxation and self-care.

- o **Exercise**: Create a daily or weekly schedule, prioritizing tasks and setting aside time for relaxation and self-care. Use tools such as to-do lists, calendars, and planners to stay organized.

7. **Social Support**: Connecting with others and seeking social support can reduce stress and promote emotional well-being. Talking to friends, family, or a therapist can provide comfort and perspective.

   - o **Exercise**: Reach out to a trusted friend or family member and share your thoughts and feelings. Consider joining a support group or seeking professional counseling if needed.

Healthy Lifestyle Choices

Making healthy lifestyle choices is essential for managing overthinking and promoting overall well-being. A balanced and healthy lifestyle supports physical, emotional, and mental health, creating a strong foundation for coping with stress and challenges.

The Importance of Healthy Lifestyle Choices

1. **Improves Physical Health**: Healthy lifestyle choices, such as a balanced diet and regular exercise, improve physical health and reduce the risk of chronic diseases. Good physical health supports overall well-being and resilience.

2. **Enhances Mental Health**: A healthy lifestyle supports mental health by reducing symptoms of anxiety and depression. It creates a positive and nurturing environment for the mind.

3. **Increases Energy Levels**: Healthy habits, such as getting enough

sleep and staying hydrated, increase energy levels and combat fatigue. This increased energy supports productivity and focus.

4. **Promotes Emotional Stability**: A balanced lifestyle promotes emotional stability by providing the body and mind with the nutrients and support they need to function optimally.

Healthy Lifestyle Choices

1. **Balanced Diet**: A balanced diet provides the body with essential nutrients and supports overall health. It helps to stabilize mood, energy levels, and cognitive function.

   o **Exercise**: Focus on eating a variety of nutrient-dense foods, including fruits, vegetables, whole grains, lean proteins, and healthy fats. Avoid excessive consumption of processed foods, sugary drinks, and high-fat snacks.

2. **Regular Exercise**: Regular exercise is crucial for physical and mental health. It improves cardiovascular health, strengthens muscles, and releases endorphins that enhance mood.

   o **Exercise**: Aim for at least 30 minutes of moderate exercise most days of the week. Choose activities that you enjoy, such as walking, cycling, swimming, or yoga, to stay motivated and consistent.

3. **Adequate Sleep**: Adequate sleep is essential for physical and mental well-being. It supports cognitive function, emotional regulation, and overall health.

   o **Exercise**: Establish a regular sleep routine by going to bed and waking up at the same time each day. Create a relaxing bedtime routine and ensure your sleep environment is comfortable and conducive to rest.

4. **Hydration**: Staying hydrated is important for overall health and energy levels. Dehydration can lead to fatigue, headaches, and difficulty concentrating.

   o **Exercise**: Drink plenty of water throughout the day. Aim for at least 8 glasses of water daily, and more if you are physically active or in a hot climate. Avoid excessive consumption of caffeine and sugary drinks.

5. **Mindful Eating**: Mindful eating involves paying attention to the experience of eating and savoring each bite. It promotes healthy

eating habits and prevents overeating.

- o **Exercise**: Practice mindful eating by slowing down and savoring each bite of your meal. Pay attention to the taste, texture, and aroma of your food. Avoid distractions such as TV or smartphones while eating.

6. **Limit Alcohol and Caffeine**: Excessive consumption of alcohol and caffeine can negatively impact physical and mental health. Moderation is key to maintaining a healthy balance.

- o **Exercise**: Limit your intake of alcohol and caffeine. If you choose to drink alcohol, do so in moderation. Opt for healthier alternatives such as herbal teas or water.

7. **Healthy Relationships**: Building and maintaining healthy

relationships is essential for emotional well-being. Positive social connections provide support, reduce stress, and enhance overall happiness.

- o **Exercise**: Nurture your relationships by spending quality time with loved ones, communicating openly, and showing appreciation. Surround yourself with supportive and positive people who uplift and inspire you.

8. **Mental Stimulation**: Keeping your mind active and engaged is important for cognitive health. Mental stimulation can enhance brain function and prevent cognitive decline.

- o **Exercise**: Engage in activities that challenge and stimulate your mind, such as reading, puzzles, learning new skills, or playing games. Stay curious and open to new experiences.

9. **Relaxation and Leisure**: Incorporating relaxation and leisure activities into your routine is essential for stress management and overall well-being. These activities provide a mental break and promote joy and relaxation.

   - **Exercise**: Set aside time each week for relaxation and leisure activities that you enjoy, such as hobbies, nature walks, or spending time with loved ones. Prioritize these activities to ensure a balanced and fulfilling life.

By incorporating self-compassion, stress management techniques, and healthy lifestyle choices into your daily routine, you can effectively manage overthinking and promote overall well-being. These practices require consistency and commitment, but with time and effort, they can lead to a more balanced, fulfilling, and mentally clear life.

6. Mindfulness and Meditation Practices

Introduction to Mindfulness

Mindfulness is the practice of being fully present and engaged in the current moment, aware of your thoughts, feelings, and sensations without judgment. This practice has its roots in Buddhist traditions and has gained significant attention in modern psychology for its benefits to mental health and overall well-being.

The Benefits of Mindfulness

1. **Reduces Stress**: Mindfulness helps to reduce stress by

promoting a state of relaxation and awareness. It allows individuals to detach from their stressors and approach them with a clearer and more balanced perspective.

2. **Enhances Emotional Regulation**: Mindfulness encourages individuals to observe their emotions without reacting impulsively. This improved emotional regulation can lead to better decision-making and healthier relationships.

3. **Improves Concentration and Focus**: By training the mind to focus on the present moment, mindfulness can enhance concentration and cognitive performance. This can be particularly beneficial in both academic and professional settings.

4. **Promotes Physical Health**: Mindfulness has been linked to

various physical health benefits, including lower blood pressure, improved sleep, and enhanced immune function.

5. **Supports Mental Health**: Regular mindfulness practice has been shown to reduce symptoms of anxiety and depression. It fosters a non-judgmental awareness that can counteract the negative thought patterns associated with these conditions.

Core Principles of Mindfulness

1. **Present Moment Awareness**: Central to mindfulness is the focus on the present moment. This means paying attention to what is happening right now, rather than ruminating on the past or worrying about the future.

2. **Non-Judgmental Observation**: Mindfulness involves observing your thoughts and feelings without labeling them as good or bad. This

helps to cultivate an attitude of acceptance and reduces the tendency to react emotionally.

3. **Acceptance**: Acceptance means acknowledging your current experience without trying to change it. This doesn't mean resignation but rather recognizing reality as it is, which can be the first step toward positive change.

4. **Patience**: Mindfulness teaches patience with yourself and the process. Recognizing that change takes time and that each moment is an opportunity to practice patience can be very grounding.

5. **Beginner's Mind**: Approaching each moment with a sense of curiosity and openness, as if you are experiencing it for the first time, helps to keep the practice fresh and engaging.

Guided Meditation Exercises

Guided meditations are structured practices led by a guide or instructor, which can be particularly helpful for beginners. These exercises can vary in length and focus, from simple breathing exercises to more complex body scans and visualization techniques.

Basic Breathing Meditation

Duration: 5-10 minutes

1. **Find a Quiet Space**: Choose a quiet and comfortable place where you won't be disturbed. Sit in a comfortable position, either on a chair with your feet flat on the ground or on a cushion with your legs crossed.

2. **Focus on Your Breath**: Close your eyes and bring your attention to your breath. Notice the sensation of the breath as it enters and leaves your nostrils, or the rise and fall of your chest or abdomen.

3. **Count Your Breaths**: To help maintain focus, you can count each breath. Inhale and silently count "one," exhale and count "two," and continue up to ten. Then start over from one.

4. **Notice Wandering Thoughts**: When your mind wanders, which it inevitably will, gently bring your focus back to your breath without judgment. Acknowledge the thought and let it go.

5. **End Gently**: After a few minutes, gently bring your awareness back to your surroundings. Open your eyes and take a moment to notice how you feel before resuming your activities.

Body Scan Meditation

Duration: 10-20 minutes

1. **Get Comfortable**: Lie down on your back with your arms at your sides, palms facing up. Close your

eyes and take a few deep breaths to relax.

2. **Begin with Your Feet**: Bring your attention to your feet. Notice any sensations in your toes, arches, and heels. Spend a few moments here before moving on.

3. **Move Up the Body**: Gradually shift your focus up through your body, spending a few moments on each area: ankles, calves, knees, thighs, hips, lower back, abdomen, chest, shoulders, arms, hands, neck, and head.

4. **Notice Sensations**: At each point, observe any sensations—tingling, warmth, tension, or relaxation. If you notice discomfort, acknowledge it without judgment and move on.

5. **Finish with Whole-Body Awareness**: Once you've scanned your entire body, take a few moments to notice how your

whole body feels. Appreciate the sense of relaxation and awareness you've cultivated.

6. **Gently Return to the Present**: When you're ready, slowly bring your awareness back to the room, wiggle your fingers and toes, and gently open your eyes.

Loving-Kindness Meditation

Duration: 10-15 minutes

1. **Find a Comfortable Position**: Sit comfortably with your back straight and your hands resting on your lap. Close your eyes and take a few deep breaths.

2. **Focus on Yourself**: Begin by silently repeating phrases of loving-kindness to yourself. Common phrases include: "May I be happy. May I be healthy. May I be safe. May I live with ease." Feel the meaning of each phrase as you repeat it.

3. **Extend to Loved Ones**: After a few minutes, bring to mind someone you care about and repeat the same phrases for them: "May you be happy. May you be healthy. May you be safe. May you live with ease."

4. **Extend to Others**: Gradually extend these wishes to others in your life, including friends, acquaintances, and even people you have difficulties with. Finally, extend loving-kindness to all beings.

5. **Feel the Connection**: As you extend loving-kindness, feel the sense of connection and compassion growing within you. Allow yourself to be open and present with these feelings.

6. **Gently End the Meditation**: When you're ready, slowly bring your awareness back to the present moment. Take a few deep breaths,

open your eyes, and notice how you feel.

Mindful Walking

Duration: 10-20 minutes

1. **Choose a Location**: Find a quiet place where you can walk undisturbed. This can be indoors or outdoors.

2. **Focus on Your Steps**: Begin walking slowly and pay attention to each step. Notice the sensation of your feet touching the ground, the movement of your legs, and the rhythm of your walking.

3. **Synchronize with Your Breath**: Coordinate your steps with your breath. For example, inhale for two steps, and exhale for two steps. Find a rhythm that feels natural.

4. **Notice Your Surroundings**: While focusing on your steps, also be aware of your surroundings. Notice the sights, sounds, and

smells around you without getting lost in thought.

5. **Observe Your Thoughts**: As thoughts arise, acknowledge them without judgment and gently bring your focus back to your walking.

6. **End Mindfully**: After your walk, take a moment to stand still and reflect on the experience. Notice how you feel physically and mentally before resuming your regular activities.

Incorporating Mindfulness into Daily Life

Mindfulness is not limited to formal meditation sessions. It can be seamlessly integrated into your daily activities, enriching your life with greater presence and awareness.

Mindful Eating

1. **Slow Down**: Eat slowly and savor each bite. Notice the flavors, textures, and aromas of your food.

2. **Eliminate Distractions**: Turn off the TV, put away your phone, and focus solely on your meal.

3. **Appreciate Your Food**: Take a moment to appreciate the effort that went into preparing your meal and the nourishment it provides.

4. **Chew Thoroughly**: Pay attention to the act of chewing and how the food changes in your mouth. This not only aids digestion but also enhances the eating experience.

Mindful Communication

1. **Active Listening**: When engaging in conversation, listen fully to the other person without planning your response while they are speaking.

2. **Observe Body Language**: Be aware of your body language and the body language of others. Notice how it complements or contrasts with the spoken words.

3. **Pause Before Responding**: Take a moment to consider your response before speaking. This can prevent impulsive or reactive comments.

4. **Express Gratitude**: Practice expressing gratitude in your interactions. Acknowledge and appreciate the efforts and kindness of others.

Mindful Work

1. **Single-Tasking**: Focus on one task at a time rather than multitasking. Give your full attention to the task at hand.

2. **Take Breaks**: Schedule regular breaks to rest and recharge. Use these breaks to practice a brief

mindfulness exercise, such as deep breathing.

3. **Set Intentions**: Begin your workday by setting clear intentions for what you hope to accomplish. This can help maintain focus and direction.

4. **End-of-Day Reflection**: Take a few minutes at the end of your workday to reflect on what you accomplished and what you can improve. Acknowledge your efforts and let go of any stress.

Mindful Routine Activities

1. **Mindful Showering**: Pay attention to the sensation of the water on your skin, the sound of the water, and the smell of the soap. Use this time as a moment of relaxation and presence.

2. **Mindful Cleaning**: When cleaning or tidying up, focus on the physical actions and the results. Notice the

transformation of your space and the satisfaction of completing the task.

3. **Mindful Commuting**: Whether you drive, bike, or walk to work, use this time to practice mindfulness. Notice the scenery, the movement of your body, and your surroundings.

4. **Mindful Waiting**: Use moments of waiting (in line, at the doctor's office, etc.) as opportunities for mindfulness. Focus on your breath or observe your surroundings without judgment.

Mindful Bedtime Routine

1. **Unplug**: Turn off electronic devices at least an hour before bed to reduce stimulation.

2. **Create a Calm Environment**: Make your bedroom a relaxing space. Dim the lights, play soothing

music, and ensure your bed is comfortable.

3. **Reflect on Your Day**: Spend a few minutes reflecting on your day. Acknowledge what went well and what you're grateful for.

4. **Practice Gratitude**: Write down or mentally note a few things you are grateful for. This can create a positive mindset before sleep.

5. **Body Scan**: Perform a quick body scan to release tension and promote relaxation before falling asleep.

By integrating mindfulness into your daily life, you can cultivate a state of continuous awareness and presence. This practice not only helps in reducing overthinking but also enhances overall well-being, making each moment more meaningful and enriching.

7. Dealing with Anxiety and Fear

Understanding Anxiety

Anxiety is a natural response to stress or perceived threats, and it can be beneficial in some situations by keeping us alert and focused. However, when anxiety becomes chronic or overwhelming, it can interfere with daily life and well-being. Understanding anxiety is the first step towards managing and overcoming it.

What Is Anxiety?

Anxiety is characterized by feelings of worry, nervousness, or fear that are strong enough to interfere with one's daily activities. It can manifest in various forms, including generalized anxiety disorder (GAD), panic disorder, social anxiety disorder, and specific phobias.

Symptoms of Anxiety

Anxiety can affect both the mind and body. Common symptoms include:

- **Emotional Symptoms**: Excessive worry, restlessness, irritability, a sense of impending doom, difficulty concentrating.

- **Physical Symptoms**: Increased heart rate, sweating, trembling, shortness of breath, dizziness, headaches, fatigue, digestive issues.

Causes of Anxiety

Anxiety can be caused by a combination of factors, including:

1. **Genetics**: A family history of anxiety or other mental health disorders can increase the risk of developing anxiety.

2. **Brain Chemistry**: Imbalances in neurotransmitters (such as serotonin, dopamine, and

norepinephrine) can contribute to anxiety.

3. **Environmental Stress**: Traumatic events, chronic stress, or significant life changes (e.g., moving, changing jobs) can trigger anxiety.

4. **Medical Conditions**: Certain medical conditions, such as thyroid disorders, heart disease, or chronic pain, can cause or exacerbate anxiety.

5. **Substance Use**: Alcohol, caffeine, and certain medications can increase anxiety symptoms.

How Anxiety Affects Daily Life

When left unmanaged, anxiety can significantly impact various aspects of life:

- **Work/School**: Difficulty concentrating and completing tasks, leading to reduced productivity and performance.

- **Relationships**: Strain on personal relationships due to irritability, withdrawal, or excessive dependence on others for reassurance.

- **Health**: Chronic anxiety can lead to physical health problems, such as cardiovascular issues, weakened immune system, and gastrointestinal disorders.

- **Mental Well-being**: Persistent anxiety can lead to depression, low self-esteem, and a reduced quality of life.

Techniques for Managing Anxiety

While anxiety can feel overwhelming, there are numerous techniques and strategies that can help manage and reduce symptoms. It is important to find what works best for you, as different methods may be more effective for different individuals.

Cognitive Behavioral Therapy (CBT)

CBT is a widely used and effective form of psychotherapy that helps individuals identify and change negative thought patterns and behaviors that contribute to anxiety.

1. **Identifying Negative Thoughts**: The first step is to become aware of the thoughts that trigger anxiety. These often include catastrophizing (expecting the worst), black-and-white thinking (seeing things as all good or all bad), and overgeneralizing (drawing broad conclusions from a single event).

2. **Challenging Negative Thoughts**: Once identified, these thoughts are challenged and reframed into more realistic and positive ones. This can be done through

questioning the evidence for and against the thought, considering alternative perspectives, and evaluating the likelihood of the feared outcome.

3. **Behavioral Techniques**: CBT also involves behavioral techniques, such as exposure therapy, where individuals gradually face their fears in a controlled and systematic way, reducing avoidance behaviors and building confidence.

Mindfulness and Relaxation Techniques

Mindfulness and relaxation techniques can help manage anxiety by promoting a sense of calm and presence.

1. **Mindfulness Meditation**: Practicing mindfulness meditation involves focusing on the present moment without judgment. This can help reduce the impact of

anxious thoughts and promote relaxation.

- **Exercise**: Find a quiet space, sit comfortably, and focus on your breath. Notice the sensation of each inhale and exhale. When your mind wanders, gently bring your attention back to your breath.

2. **Deep Breathing**: Deep breathing exercises can activate the body's relaxation response, reducing the physical symptoms of anxiety.

- **Exercise**: Sit or lie down comfortably. Inhale deeply through your nose for a count of four, hold for a count of four, and exhale slowly through your mouth for a count of six. Repeat several times.

3. **Progressive Muscle Relaxation**: This technique involves tensing

and then relaxing different muscle groups to release physical tension.

- o **Exercise**: Starting with your feet, tense the muscles as tightly as possible, hold for a few seconds, and then release. Move up through your body, tensing and relaxing each muscle group.

Lifestyle Changes

Making certain lifestyle changes can have a significant impact on managing anxiety.

1. **Regular Exercise**: Physical activity releases endorphins, which can improve mood and reduce anxiety.

   - o **Exercise**: Aim for at least 30 minutes of moderate exercise most days of the week. Activities like walking, jogging, yoga, and swimming can be particularly beneficial.

2. **Healthy Diet**: Eating a balanced diet can affect overall mental health and help manage anxiety.

   o **Diet Tips**: Focus on whole foods, such as fruits, vegetables, lean proteins, and whole grains. Avoid excessive caffeine and sugar, which can exacerbate anxiety symptoms.

3. **Adequate Sleep**: Quality sleep is crucial for mental and emotional well-being.

   o **Sleep Tips**: Establish a regular sleep routine, create a relaxing bedtime ritual, and ensure your sleep environment is comfortable and free from distractions.

4. **Limiting Alcohol and Caffeine**: Both alcohol and caffeine can increase anxiety and interfere with sleep.

- o **Tips**: Reduce or eliminate consumption of these substances, especially if you notice they contribute to your anxiety.

Building a Support System

Having a strong support system can provide emotional support and practical assistance in managing anxiety.

1. **Friends and Family**: Share your experiences and feelings with trusted friends and family members. Their understanding and support can be invaluable.

2. **Support Groups**: Consider joining a support group for individuals with anxiety. Sharing experiences and coping strategies with others who understand can be comforting and empowering.

3. **Professional Help**: Don't hesitate to seek help from a mental health professional. Therapists,

counselors, and psychiatrists can provide valuable guidance and treatment options.

Facing and Overcoming Fears

One of the most challenging aspects of anxiety is facing and overcoming fears. However, with the right approach and support, it is possible to confront and manage these fears effectively.

Understanding Your Fears

The first step in overcoming fears is to understand them. This involves identifying what you are afraid of and why. Consider the following questions:

- **What am I afraid of?**: Clearly define your fear. Is it a specific situation, object, or activity?

- **Why am I afraid?**: Reflect on the underlying reasons for your fear.

Is it based on a past experience, a perceived threat, or an irrational belief?

- **How does this fear affect me?**: Consider how your fear impacts your daily life, relationships, and well-being.

Gradual Exposure

Exposure therapy is a highly effective technique for overcoming fears. It involves gradually and systematically exposing yourself to the feared object or situation in a controlled way.

1. **Create a Fear Hierarchy**: List your fears from least to most frightening. For example, if you have a fear of public speaking, your list might start with speaking in front of a small group of friends and end with giving a presentation to a large audience.

2. **Start Small**: Begin with the least frightening item on your list.

Expose yourself to this fear in a controlled and safe environment. Use relaxation techniques to manage anxiety during exposure.

3. **Increase Exposure Gradually**: Once you feel comfortable with the first item, move on to the next. Gradually increase the level of exposure, allowing yourself to build confidence and reduce fear at each step.

4. **Practice Regularly**: Consistent practice is key to overcoming fears. Regularly expose yourself to the feared situation, gradually increasing the difficulty level.

Cognitive Restructuring

Cognitive restructuring involves identifying and challenging irrational or unhelpful thoughts related to your fears.

1. **Identify Negative Thoughts**: Pay attention to the thoughts that arise when you think about or

encounter your fear. Write them down.

2. **Challenge Negative Thoughts**: Evaluate the evidence for and against these thoughts. Are they based on facts or assumptions? What is the worst that could happen, and how likely is it?

3. **Replace with Positive Thoughts**: Replace irrational thoughts with more realistic and positive ones. For example, if you fear flying, instead of thinking, "The plane will crash," think, "Flying is statistically very safe, and thousands of flights happen safely every day."

Building Resilience

Building resilience can help you manage and overcome fears more effectively. Resilience involves developing the mental and emotional strength to cope with stress and adversity.

1. **Develop a Positive Mindset**: Focus on your strengths and achievements. Practice self-compassion and positive self-talk.

2. **Set Realistic Goals**: Set achievable goals and take small steps towards them. Celebrate your progress, no matter how small.

3. **Practice Problem-Solving**: Develop your problem-solving skills to effectively tackle challenges and obstacles.

4. **Stay Connected**: Maintain strong social connections and seek support when needed. Sharing your experiences with others can provide perspective and encouragement.

Seeking Professional Help

If your fears are significantly impacting your life and you find it difficult to manage them on your own, consider seeking help from a mental health professional. Therapists and counselors can provide specialized techniques and support for overcoming fears.

1. **Cognitive Behavioral Therapy (CBT)**: CBT is effective for treating a wide range of anxiety disorders and specific phobias. It helps individuals identify and change negative thought patterns and behaviors.

2. **Exposure Therapy**: A therapist can guide you through exposure therapy, providing support and techniques to manage anxiety during the process.

3. **Medication**: In some cases, medication may be prescribed to help manage anxiety symptoms. This can be used in conjunction with therapy for better results.

8. Creating a Support System

The Importance of Social Support

Social support plays a crucial role in maintaining mental health and overall well-being. It involves having a network of family, friends, and community members who provide emotional, informational, and practical assistance. Strong social support can buffer the effects of stress, enhance resilience, and improve life satisfaction.

Types of Social Support

1. **Emotional Support**: This includes empathy, love, trust, and caring. Emotional support involves listening and providing comfort and reassurance during times of stress or difficulty.

2. **Instrumental Support**: This involves providing tangible assistance, such as financial help, transportation, or help with daily tasks.

3. **Informational Support**: This includes providing advice, suggestions, and information that can help someone solve problems or make decisions.

4. **Appraisal Support**: This involves providing feedback and affirmation that helps someone understand and assess their situation and options.

Benefits of Social Support

1. **Stress Reduction**: Social support helps to reduce stress by providing a sense of security and belonging. Knowing that you have people to turn to during challenging times can alleviate feelings of loneliness and anxiety.

2. **Improved Mental Health**: Strong social connections are associated with lower rates of depression, anxiety, and other mental health issues. Emotional support from loved ones can boost self-esteem and promote a positive outlook on life.

3. **Enhanced Coping Skills**: Having a supportive network can improve your ability to cope with difficult situations. Friends and family can offer different perspectives, practical advice, and emotional encouragement.

4. **Better Physical Health**: Social support is linked to better physical health outcomes, including lower blood pressure, improved immune function, and a reduced risk of chronic diseases. Positive relationships can also encourage healthy behaviors, such as regular exercise and a balanced diet.

5. **Longevity**: Studies have shown that people with strong social networks tend to live longer. The sense of connection and purpose that comes from relationships can contribute to a longer, healthier life.

Building and Maintaining Social Support

1. **Invest in Relationships**: Building strong relationships takes time and effort. Regularly reach out to friends and family, spend quality time together, and show appreciation for their support.

2. **Communicate Openly**: Open and honest communication is key to maintaining healthy relationships. Share your thoughts and feelings, listen actively, and be supportive of others.

3. **Be Available**: Offer your time and assistance to others. Being reliable and dependable strengthens your

relationships and ensures that your support network is reciprocal.

4. **Join Groups and Activities**: Participate in social groups, clubs, or activities that interest you. This can help you meet new people and expand your social network.

5. **Seek Professional Support**: If you're struggling to build or maintain relationships, consider seeking help from a therapist or counselor. They can provide guidance and strategies for improving your social connections.

Building Healthy Relationships

Healthy relationships are a cornerstone of well-being. They provide emotional support, companionship, and a sense of belonging. Building and maintaining healthy relationships requires effort, communication, and mutual respect.

Characteristics of Healthy Relationships

1. **Mutual Respect**: Respecting each other's boundaries, opinions, and individuality is essential for a healthy relationship. Mutual respect fosters trust and reduces conflict.

2. **Open Communication**: Effective communication involves both speaking and listening. It's important to express your thoughts and feelings honestly and to listen actively to your partner or friend.

3. **Trust**: Trust is the foundation of any healthy relationship. It involves being reliable, honest, and consistent in your actions and words.

4. **Support**: Providing and receiving support in times of need strengthens relationships. This includes emotional support, practical assistance, and encouragement.

5. **Equality**: Healthy relationships are balanced, with both parties having an equal say and feeling valued. Power imbalances can lead to resentment and conflict.

6. **Healthy Boundaries**: Setting and respecting boundaries ensures that both parties feel comfortable and safe. Boundaries can involve personal space, time, and emotional limits.

Building Healthy Relationships

1. **Develop Self-Awareness**: Understanding your own needs, values, and boundaries is the first step in building healthy relationships. Self-awareness allows you to communicate more

effectively and to choose relationships that align with your values.

2. **Communicate Effectively**: Practice active listening, express your thoughts and feelings clearly, and be open to feedback. Effective communication helps to resolve conflicts and build trust.

3. **Show Appreciation**: Regularly express gratitude and appreciation for your partner or friend. Acknowledging their positive qualities and actions strengthens your bond.

4. **Spend Quality Time Together**: Make time for shared activities and experiences. Whether it's a date night, a weekend getaway, or a simple walk in the park, spending quality time together fosters connection.

5. **Be Supportive**: Offer your support in times of need and celebrate each

other's successes. Being there for each other strengthens your relationship.

6. **Resolve Conflicts Constructively**: Disagreements are a natural part of any relationship. It's important to address conflicts calmly and respectfully, focusing on finding solutions rather than assigning blame.

Maintaining Healthy Relationships

1. **Regular Check-Ins**: Schedule regular check-ins with your partner or friend to discuss your relationship and address any issues. This can help prevent misunderstandings and ensure that both parties feel heard.

2. **Respect Boundaries**: Continually respect each other's boundaries and be willing to adjust them as needed. Boundaries can change over time, and it's important to communicate any changes.

3. **Keep the Romance Alive**: In romantic relationships, make an effort to keep the romance alive. Small gestures, such as surprise notes or thoughtful gifts, can keep the spark alive.

4. **Seek Balance**: Ensure that your relationship is balanced and that both parties feel valued and appreciated. Avoid power imbalances and strive for equality.

5. **Be Adaptable**: Relationships evolve over time, and it's important to be adaptable. Be open to change and willing to grow together.

Seeking Professional Help When Needed

While social support and healthy relationships are crucial, there are times when professional help is necessary. Seeking help from a mental health professional can provide valuable guidance, support, and treatment for various mental health issues.

When to Seek Professional Help

1. **Persistent Anxiety or Depression**: If you experience persistent feelings of anxiety or depression that interfere with your daily life, it's important to seek professional help. A mental health professional can provide therapy and, if necessary, medication.

2. **Trauma or Grief**: Experiencing trauma or the loss of a loved one can be overwhelming. Professional support can help you process your emotions and develop healthy coping strategies.

3. **Relationship Issues**: If you're struggling with relationship issues, such as communication problems, trust issues, or conflict, couples therapy or individual therapy can

provide valuable insights and tools for improvement.

4. **Substance Abuse**: If you're struggling with substance abuse, professional help is essential. Addiction is a complex issue that requires specialized treatment and support.

5. **Severe Stress**: Chronic stress can have serious physical and mental health consequences. A mental health professional can help you develop effective stress management techniques.

6. **Behavioral Changes**: If you notice significant changes in your behavior, such as withdrawing from social activities, changes in sleep or eating patterns, or increased irritability, it's important to seek help.

Types of Professional Help

1. **Therapy and Counseling**: Therapy and counseling involve talking with a trained mental health professional to address emotional and psychological issues. There are various types of therapy, including cognitive-behavioral therapy (CBT), psychodynamic therapy, and humanistic therapy.

2. **Psychiatry**: Psychiatrists are medical doctors who specialize in mental health. They can diagnose mental health conditions and prescribe medication if needed. Psychiatry is often used in conjunction with therapy for comprehensive treatment.

3. **Support Groups**: Support groups provide a space for individuals to share their experiences and receive support from others facing similar challenges. Support groups can be particularly helpful for

issues such as addiction, grief, and chronic illness.

4. **Crisis Intervention**: Crisis intervention services provide immediate support for individuals experiencing a mental health crisis. This can include hotlines, emergency counseling, and hospitalization if necessary.

5. **Holistic Therapies**: Holistic therapies, such as mindfulness, yoga, and acupuncture, can complement traditional mental health treatments. These therapies focus on the mind-body connection and can help reduce stress and promote overall well-being.

Finding the Right Professional

1. **Research**: Research potential therapists, counselors, and psychiatrists. Look for professionals who specialize in the issues you're facing and have

positive reviews or recommendations.

2. **Credentials and Experience**: Ensure that the professional you choose is licensed and has the necessary credentials and experience. This information is often available on their website or through professional directories.

3. **Compatibility**: It's important to find a mental health professional with whom you feel comfortable. Don't hesitate to schedule a consultation to see if they are a good fit for you.

4. **Ask for Recommendations**: Ask friends, family, or your primary care doctor for recommendations. Personal referrals can be a valuable resource.

5. **Consider Practical Factors**: Consider practical factors such as location, cost, and availability. Ensure that the professional's

office is conveniently located and that their fees are within your budget.

Making the Most of Professional Help

1. **Be Open and Honest**: Be open and honest with your mental health professional. Share your thoughts, feelings, and experiences fully to get the most out of your sessions.

2. **Set Goals**: Work with your therapist to set clear, achievable goals for your treatment. This can help you stay focused and track your progress.

3. **Follow Through**: Follow through with any homework or exercises assigned by your therapist. Consistent effort is key to making progress.

4. **Be Patient**: Healing and growth take time. Be patient with yourself

and the process, and trust that you will see improvement over time.

5. **Advocate for Yourself**: If you feel that a particular approach isn't working, don't hesitate to discuss it with your therapist. Advocating for yourself ensures that you receive the best possible care.

9. Long-Term Strategies for Mental Wellness

Developing Positive Habits

Habits are the building blocks of our daily lives, influencing our actions, decisions, and overall well-being. Developing positive habits can significantly enhance our quality of life, leading to improved mental health, productivity, and satisfaction. Positive habits are consistent behaviors that contribute to your physical, emotional, and mental health.

The Science of Habit Formation

Understanding how habits are formed can help in developing positive ones. According to research, habits form through a process called the habit loop, which consists of three key components:

1. **Cue**: This is a trigger that initiates the behavior. It can be a specific time of day, an emotional state, or a particular location.

2. **Routine**: This is the behavior itself. It is the action you want to turn into a habit.

3. **Reward**: This is the positive outcome you experience from performing the behavior, which reinforces the habit.

Steps to Developing Positive Habits

1. **Start Small**: Begin with small, manageable changes. Trying to overhaul your life overnight can be overwhelming and unsustainable.

2. **Set Clear Goals**: Define specific, measurable, achievable, relevant, and time-bound (SMART) goals. Clear goals provide direction and motivation.

3. **Create a Routine**: Establish a consistent routine. Perform the desired behavior at the same time and in the same context every day to strengthen the habit loop.

4. **Use Triggers**: Identify and use specific cues to remind you to perform the behavior. For example, placing your workout clothes next to your bed can remind you to exercise in the morning.

5. **Reward Yourself**: Reinforce the habit by rewarding yourself after completing the behavior. Rewards

can be intrinsic (e.g., feeling accomplished) or extrinsic (e.g., a small treat).

6. **Track Your Progress**: Keep a journal or use an app to track your progress. Monitoring your behavior helps to stay accountable and recognize improvements.

7. **Be Patient**: Habits take time to form. Research suggests it can take anywhere from 18 to 254 days to form a new habit, with an average of 66 days. Be patient and persistent.

Examples of Positive Habits

1. **Healthy Eating**: Develop habits such as preparing meals in advance, incorporating more fruits and vegetables into your diet, and reducing processed food intake.

2. **Regular Exercise**: Aim for at least 30 minutes of physical activity most days of the week. Find an

exercise routine that you enjoy to make it more sustainable.

3. **Mindfulness Practices**: Incorporate mindfulness activities like meditation, deep breathing exercises, or yoga into your daily routine to reduce stress and improve mental clarity.

4. **Adequate Sleep**: Establish a consistent sleep schedule, create a relaxing bedtime routine, and ensure your sleep environment is conducive to rest.

5. **Continuous Learning**: Dedicate time each day to read, take online courses, or engage in activities that promote intellectual growth.

Continual Learning and Self-Improvement

Lifelong learning and self-improvement are essential for personal and professional growth. Continual learning involves actively seeking new knowledge, skills, and experiences throughout your life. Self-improvement focuses on enhancing various aspects of your life to achieve your full potential.

Benefits of Continual Learning

1. **Adaptability**: Continual learning enhances your ability to adapt to new situations and challenges. It keeps your mind sharp and prepares you for changes in your personal and professional life.

2. **Career Advancement**: Acquiring new skills and knowledge can lead to better job opportunities, promotions, and increased job satisfaction.

3. **Personal Growth**: Learning new things can boost your self-esteem, confidence, and overall sense of accomplishment. It encourages you to step out of your comfort zone and grow.

4. **Improved Mental Health**: Engaging in learning activities can reduce stress, improve cognitive function, and delay the onset of cognitive decline associated with aging.

5. **Social Connections**: Learning often involves interacting with others, whether through classes, workshops, or study groups. This can help you build new relationships and expand your social network.

Strategies for Continual Learning

1. **Set Learning Goals**: Identify areas you want to improve or new skills you want to acquire. Set specific, achievable goals to guide your learning journey.

2. **Utilize Online Resources**: Take advantage of online courses, webinars, and tutorials. Platforms like Coursera, Udemy, and Khan

Academy offer a wide range of topics.

3. **Read Regularly**: Make reading a habit. Choose books, articles, and journals that interest you and expand your knowledge. Set aside time each day for reading.

4. **Attend Workshops and Seminars**: Participate in workshops, seminars, and conferences related to your interests or profession. These events provide valuable learning opportunities and networking.

5. **Practice and Apply**: Put what you learn into practice. Apply new skills and knowledge in real-life situations to reinforce learning and gain practical experience.

6. **Seek Feedback**: Ask for feedback from mentors, peers, or supervisors. Constructive feedback helps you identify areas for

improvement and refine your skills.

7. **Reflect on Your Learning**: Regularly reflect on what you have learned and how you can apply it. Reflection helps consolidate knowledge and identify further learning needs.

Self-Improvement Practices

1. **Self-Reflection**: Regularly take time to reflect on your thoughts, behaviors, and goals. Self-reflection helps you gain insight into your strengths and areas for improvement.

2. **Set Personal Goals**: Identify specific, meaningful goals that align with your values and aspirations. Break them down into actionable steps and track your progress.

3. **Develop a Growth Mindset**: Embrace a mindset that values

learning and growth. Believe in your ability to improve and view challenges as opportunities for development.

4. **Seek Out Challenges**: Step out of your comfort zone and take on new challenges. Challenges provide opportunities for growth and help build resilience.

5. **Build Resilience**: Develop coping strategies to manage stress and adversity. Practices such as mindfulness, exercise, and maintaining a strong support network can enhance resilience.

6. **Cultivate Positive Habits**: Focus on building habits that contribute to your overall well-being, such as regular exercise, healthy eating, and adequate sleep.

7. **Prioritize Self-Care**: Make time for activities that nourish your mind, body, and spirit. Self-care is

essential for maintaining balance and preventing burnout.

Maintaining a Balanced Life

Maintaining a balanced life involves managing various aspects of your life in a way that promotes overall well-being and satisfaction. A balanced life allows you to fulfill your responsibilities, pursue your interests, and nurture your physical and mental health.

Components of a Balanced Life

1. **Work-Life Balance**: Balance your professional responsibilities with personal time and activities. This involves setting boundaries, managing your time effectively, and prioritizing self-care.

2. **Physical Health**: Take care of your body through regular exercise, a balanced diet, adequate sleep, and preventive healthcare.

3. **Mental and Emotional Health**: Prioritize your mental and emotional well-being by managing stress, practicing mindfulness, and seeking support when needed.

4. **Social Connections**: Nurture relationships with family, friends, and your community. Social connections provide support, companionship, and a sense of belonging.

5. **Personal Growth**: Dedicate time to personal development and self-improvement. Continual learning and setting personal goals contribute to a sense of fulfillment.

6. **Leisure and Recreation**: Engage in hobbies and activities that you enjoy. Leisure time is important for relaxation and rejuvenation.

7. **Spirituality**: For many people, spirituality or a sense of purpose is an important aspect of life. This can involve religious practices,

meditation, or finding meaning in daily activities.

Strategies for Maintaining Balance

1. **Set Priorities**: Identify your values and priorities. Focus on what is most important to you and allocate your time and energy accordingly.

2. **Create a Schedule**: Plan your day and week to ensure you have time for work, self-care, and leisure. Use tools like calendars and to-do lists to stay organized.

3. **Learn to Say No**: Set boundaries and say no to commitments that do not align with your priorities or that overwhelm you. It's important to protect your time and energy.

4. **Practice Time Management**: Use time management techniques, such as the Pomodoro Technique or time blocking, to stay focused and productive.

5. **Delegate and Seek Help**: Don't be afraid to delegate tasks or seek help when needed. Sharing responsibilities can reduce stress and free up time for other activities.

6. **Take Breaks**: Incorporate regular breaks into your day to rest and recharge. Short breaks can improve productivity and prevent burnout.

7. **Reflect and Adjust**: Regularly reflect on your life balance and make adjustments as needed. Life circumstances and priorities can change, and it's important to adapt.

Overcoming Obstacles to Balance

1. **Manage Stress**: Develop effective stress management techniques, such as deep breathing exercises, mindfulness meditation, and physical activity.

2. **Address Burnout**: Recognize the signs of burnout, such as fatigue, irritability, and reduced performance. Take steps to address burnout by prioritizing self-care and seeking support.

3. **Avoid Perfectionism**: Strive for progress, not perfection. Perfectionism can lead to unnecessary stress and hinder your ability to enjoy life.

4. **Stay Flexible**: Be open to change and adapt to new circumstances. Flexibility allows you to maintain balance even when faced with unexpected challenges.

5. **Seek Professional Help**: If you're struggling to maintain balance, consider seeking help from a therapist or counselor. Professional support can provide valuable insights and strategies.

11. Conclusion

Recap of Key Points

Throughout this book, we've explored various strategies and techniques to help you stop overthinking and lead a more balanced, fulfilling life. Here's a brief recap of the key points covered:

1. **Understanding Overthinking**: Recognizing the signs and consequences of overthinking and understanding its impact on mental health and daily life.

2. **The Science Behind Overthinking**: Exploring the psychological and neurological basis of overthinking.

3. **Common Triggers and Causes**: Identifying the factors that

contribute to overthinking and learning how to manage them.

4. **Recognizing the Signs of Overthinking**: Understanding the symptoms and behaviors associated with overthinking.

5. **Mindfulness and Awareness**: Using mindfulness practices to stay present and reduce overthinking.

6. **Cognitive Behavioral Techniques**: Implementing CBT methods to challenge and change overthinking patterns.

7. **Developing a Growth Mindset**: Cultivating a mindset that embraces challenges and learning opportunities.

8. **The Power of Journaling**: Using journaling as a tool for self-reflection and reducing overthinking.

9. **Setting Boundaries and Priorities**: Learning to set boundaries and prioritize tasks to reduce stress.

10. **Time Management and Productivity Tips**: Applying effective time management strategies to enhance productivity.

11. **The Role of Self-Compassion**: Practicing self-compassion to alleviate self-criticism and overthinking.

12. **Stress Management Techniques**: Utilizing stress management methods to maintain mental and emotional well-being.

13. **Healthy Lifestyle Choices**: Adopting healthy habits to support overall well-being.

14. **Introduction to Mindfulness**: Learning about mindfulness and its benefits.

15. **Guided Meditation Exercises**: Incorporating guided meditation into your routine to reduce stress and overthinking.

16. **Incorporating Mindfulness into Daily Life**: Making mindfulness a part of your everyday activities.

17. **Understanding Anxiety**: Recognizing the relationship between anxiety and overthinking.

18. **Techniques for Managing Anxiety**: Implementing strategies to manage anxiety effectively.

19. **Facing and Overcoming Fears**: Building resilience by facing and overcoming fears.

20. **The Importance of Social Support**: Recognizing the value of social support in maintaining mental health.

21. **Building Healthy Relationships**: Developing and nurturing healthy relationships.

22. **Seeking Professional Help When Needed**: Knowing when to seek professional support for mental health issues.

23. **Developing Positive Habits**: Establishing and maintaining positive habits for overall well-being.

24. **Continual Learning and Self-Improvement**: Committing to lifelong learning and personal growth.

25. **Maintaining a Balanced Life**: Strategies for achieving and maintaining a balanced life.

Encouragement for the Future

Embarking on the journey to stop overthinking and improve your mental well-being is a significant and commendable step. It requires commitment, patience, and perseverance. Remember, change doesn't happen overnight, but every small step you take brings you closer to your goal. Celebrate your progress, no matter how small, and be kind to yourself along the way.

Keep in mind that it's normal to face setbacks and challenges. What matters is how you respond to them. Use the techniques and strategies outlined in this book to navigate through difficult times. Surround yourself with supportive people, and don't hesitate to seek professional help if needed.

Stay committed to your journey of self-improvement. Continually seek new knowledge, develop positive habits, and strive for balance in all areas of your life. By doing so, you will build resilience, reduce overthinking, and enhance your overall well-being.

Final Thoughts

In conclusion, overthinking can significantly impact your quality of life, but with the right tools and mindset, you can overcome it. This book has provided you with a comprehensive guide to understanding, managing, and reducing overthinking. By implementing the strategies discussed, you can develop healthier thought patterns, improve your mental health, and lead a more balanced and fulfilling life.

Remember, the journey to stop overthinking is ongoing, and it's essential to be patient with yourself. Embrace the process of learning and growth, and continue to apply the techniques that work best for you. With determination and persistence, you can break free from the cycle of overthinking and enjoy a more peaceful, focused, and happy life.

Thank you for taking this journey with us. We wish you all the best in your pursuit of mental clarity, emotional well-being, and a balanced life.

Stop Overthinking

R. Sharma

Author's Message

As you turn the final page of "Stop Overthinking: Master Your Mind, Reduce Stress, and Live a Happier Life," I want to leave you with a heartfelt message. This journey you've embarked on is a testament to your courage and commitment to personal growth. Remember, you have the power to change your thoughts and, in turn, your life.

Overthinking may have been a familiar companion, but it doesn't define you. Each step you take towards mindfulness, self-compassion, and mental clarity is a victory. Celebrate your progress, no matter how small, and be gentle with yourself in moments of struggle.

Life is a beautiful balance of challenges and joys. Embrace each moment with an open heart, knowing that you have the tools to navigate whatever comes your way. Trust in your resilience, and remember that every day is an opportunity to create a more peaceful and fulfilling life.

Thank you for allowing me to be a part of your journey. May you continue to find strength, peace, and happiness as you master your mind and embrace the present.

With gratitude and best wishes,

R. Sharma